John O. Coit

**The Religion of Manhood**

John O. Coit

**The Religion of Manhood**

ISBN/EAN: 9783337725549

Printed in Europe, USA, Canada, Australia, Japan

Cover: Foto ©Lupo / pixelio.de

More available books at **www.hansebooks.com**

# The Religion of Manhood:

By John Owen Coit

Author of "Inspirations," and "One Man's Thesis" : : :

G. P. Putnam's Sons
New York: 27 West 23d St.
London: 24 Bedford St., Strand
The Knickerbocker Press : : 1896

COPYRIGHT, 1896
BY
JOHN OWEN COIT
*Entered at Stationers' Hall, London*

# ACKNOWLEDGMENT.

Acknowledgment is hereby made to the owners of the copyrights of the quotations contained in Part II. of this little work, for their courtesy in granting permission for the use of the same.

Special thanks are due to Mrs. A. D. T. Whitney, Mrs. Julia Ditto Young, Miss Edith M. Thomas, Lewis Morris, William Watson, L. E. Mosher, the Bridgeport *Standard*, the Los Angeles *Times*, the Chicago *Times-Herald*, and Messrs. Charles Scribner's Sons, Henry Holt & Co., Houghton, Mifflin & Co., Smith, Elder & Co.

J. O. C.

# CONTENTS.

## PART I.

|  | PAGE |
|---|---|
| SUPPORT | 3 |
| OUR DESTINED PART | 4 |
| IN REALITY | 6 |
| WITH BELIEF | 9 |
| THE ABIDING INFLUENCE | 12 |
| DEATH | 12 |
| THE LIFE WHICH IS MORE THAN MEAT | 13 |
| THE LIFE BEYOND | 14 |
| RELIGIOUS EVOLUTION | 14 |
| UPWARD | 15 |
| QUESTIONS AS TO GOD | 16 |
| FAITH AND REASON | 17 |
| "HEATHENISM" AND CHURCH-ATTENDANCE | 18 |
| TO BE A CHRISTIAN | 19 |
| WITHOUT GOD | 20 |
| FEAR | 22 |

## Contents

| | PAGE |
|---|---|
| UNHAPPINESS | 23 |
| THE SICKNESS OF OVERWORK | 24 |
| SELF-HELP | 24 |
| TO BENEFIT | 25 |
| PROGRESS O'ER THE SANDS | 25 |
| AS TO COMPLETED RESULTS | 25 |
| STRENGTH, SIMPLICITY ; TRUTH, PURITY | 26 |
| THE SPIRIT LIFE, WHAT IS IT ? | 27 |
| THE GOODNESS OF GOD | 28 |
| A WRITER'S LIFE | 29 |
| CONTENT | 30 |
| LITERAL CHRISTIANITY | 31 |
| WHAT IS THE SOUL ? | 31 |
| EARTH'S MESSAGE | 32 |
| AFTERWARD | 33 |
| TO REV. JOHN HUTCHINS | 34 |
| TWO PICTURES | 35 |
| HOW TO LIVE | 37 |
| A CONQUEROR | 37 |
| WHAT IS SIN ? | 38 |
| A PRAYER | 38 |
| A STATEMENT | 39 |
| AN ANSWER TO "ISOLATION OF INDIVIDUALITY" | 39 |
| EVIL IS BUT PERVERTED GOOD | 41 |

## PART II.

PAGE

QUOTATIONS AND SUGGESTIONS . . . 45

### SUMMARY.

RELIGION . . . . . . . 96
SACRIFICE . . . . . . . 98

## PART I.

## ESSAYS AND POEMS.

# THE RELIGION OF MANHOOD.

## *Support.*

ONE who has tasted the delights of the heights, and suffered the agonies of the depths, knows that a balanced life is the ideal one, a life in which the trials and sufferings of one time are offset and counterbalanced by delights and compensations at other times, in such ways that humanity is better adjusted, the divinity of man is better apprehended, and the fact that God is infinite is somewhat comprehended.

We cannot go further or wider than this, as a foundation, without insanity. We cannot go less far or less wide without sacrificing that completeness which it is possible for each of us to give to his or her life.

Not but that many men can and do live, unto the end, on a narrower foundation than this. Not but that many men seem to consider themselves and their own lives sufficiently complete without such a foundation, but let us judge their lives impartially, compare them with the lives of greater men, notice the incompleteness of the lesser lives, then ask ourselves if we are willing to continue to live below our rightful plane, unsupported by faith in and realization of a higher, truer, nobler life, as indicated by the lines below?

"A life which stands as all true lives have stood,
Firm rooted in the faith that God is good."

### *Our Destined Part.*

It makes little difference whether we call this higher, truer, nobler influence, in our lives and in the world, God, or Fate, or Destiny, but it is important, vitally important, as to whether we do or do not believe in some such force, of which we are a part and to which we go, at the end.

The "end, beginning, mean, and end to all things," the life-giving influence, that is the influence for us to choose and hold to, omitting the lesser and lower, because " The Life " is " more than meat," therefore the lesser things of this life should be subordinated, and kept in their true places, underneath, not in the first place in our thoughts. Not neglecting the less important matters, but keeping them in their relative position, under, not above, for

—above all treasures is thy soul's good, endlessly :

Yet we should not put our own pleasure, nor even our spiritual profit in advance of real, practical work for others, for only through the working of natural laws are these better things to be accomplished, only by labor for the good of others are the best results attained, in life and in character.

Not but that our own pleasure may and will be, to a great extent, included in our work for others, but our own pleasure must not be the first object in our view. Instead, it should be at least secondary, else we will fail in our efforts to win that which is best worth winning, and will fail to accomplish that which is most worth accomplishing.

### *In Reality.*

After all, it is not a question of fame, honor, money, or opinion, but a question as to the reality of these higher influences, the lesser and greater of these subtler influences which make men gentlemen, and which refine, elevate, and improve us and our standards. Are they, as we are sometimes tempted to believe, all imagination, or are they, indeed, the most real of all?

Are we, in our souls, but passing influences, or are we in our higher selves part of God?

Bryant has written,—

"—surrendering up thine individual being
Shalt thou go to mix forever with the
elements,

To be a brother to the insensible rock,
And to the clod,—"

"Never," my spirit says to me, as clearly as any words fall on the natural ear, "never to be a rock or a clod, or any such gross and lifeless thing!" The body, the lesser, lower self, may and indeed will perish, but the soul will then be free from all sin, pain, and sorsow, and all narrow limits.

Why should I be, in any way, afraid of death? "Answer the testimony of the life, if you can, you who doubt," we are told ; and the continual testimony of my life has been to teach me, at least, the reality of spirituality, and the unsatisfying ability of earthly things. Why is it that I have been so continually unable to settle down to business? Why is it that I have, at times, thought so lightly of money-making? Has it not been because,

"I have seen higher, holier things than these,

And therefore must to these refuse my heart"?

I have dreaded "love of money" ever since I began to realize what sordid creatures most money-makers become, except where the growing fondness for money and its purchasing power is well balanced by a good love for family or friends. I have desired to so "bear witness" that others would be more truly benefited than if I gave myself with absorbing interest to the money-getting which has become so necessary a part of our modern life and welfare, if one would keep any respectable place in civilization. Is modern civilization right in its present view of position,—position as held by man's material power, rather than by a man's worth as a man, and by his power for good in higher than material lines? Surely modern civilization is not right as to parts of these subjects, yet we cannot improve matters except as we improve ourselves, gain the ear of modern civilization, and say to it, "Look higher!"

Is not the power of a good, true and noble life to be found to-day, just as Lowell described it, as applied to " earth's chosen heroes," not in the yielding to popular fallacies, but in living as men should live? To do this, let us realize, in and through ourselves, the ideal presented by Thomas Hughes, when he says: "Courage is the foundation of manliness; and manliness is the perfection of character."

### *With Belief.*

It is not a question of "How can I believe in God?" It is a question of "How can I, even if I would, disbelieve in Him?"

Some men, men who have lived through less than I have, men who are obliged to judge from a surface or shallow or small experience of life, may wonder why I so intensely, so vitally, so thoroughly believe; but those who have been through more nearly similar experiences, those who have suffered, those who have been up and down, well and sick, happy and sad, disappointed, tried, harassed, and then, in turn, elevated in spirit almost beyond what reasonable life can bear—these men will realize that there is a God working in and through us, a vital force which is more than nature, or imagination, or chance, or fate, or intellect!

" The sun doth not contain Him, nor the sea,"—that is, neither one of these is sufficient to comprehend Him, although He is, indeed, working ever, in and through nature and nature's law.

No chance, no fate, would have been, I believe, persistent enough to have overruled me in the ways in which I have been overruled, continually. I find, instead, a purpose in it all, a calling to look higher, a plan of God, an evidence that He loves all, and because of that love does not shrink from causing pain, for future good.

We are told, and told truly, that as to human love,

"—that love is false which clings to love
For selfish sweets of love."

May not the same be true, yes, may it not be even more true as to the Divine love? God allows us, for His own infinite cause, to suffer, to doubt, and even to fall, but later He may reveal more of His reasons, at least we shall be sufficiently sustained, encouraged and delivered, if we but consistently act up to our own best ideals and knowledge of results, as they become revealed to us. Is it not enough, for the present, to know that God loves us, to know that the great power of this earth, the all-directing Destiny, is good and not evil, and that, as a natural result, the outcome will be good?

Let not the knowledge referred to in the last paragraph, be taken as excusing a lack of personal application! God has, so far, in all our later history, acted through men, not angels, so it is very important that each one take up and bear, continually, his or her burden of work and assistance in the great plans now going forward, the plans for the enlightenment and improvement of our age, our lives and characters, and those of the nations with which we all come into more or less communication, according to our own wills and willingness.

### *The Abiding Influence.*

It may be slow,
 It must be sure;
Elsewise your work
 Will not endure.

### *Death.*

When our shade falls, the messenger will come with shining face
To lead us from earth's valley to the palace of God's grace,
Where loved ones gone before us still live, and love, and pray;
Where no night cometh, ever, and no heat blights the day.

Shall we go forth with trembling, with sorrow, or with woe?
Shall we not trust that mercy which led us here below?
Shall we not trust our loved ones to the God who rules o'erhead?
Will He not keep them truly, giving them their daily bread?

*The Life Which is More than Meat.*

Oh, this spirit-life! So true, so real, so vital, and yet so intangible when we wish, literally, to grasp it! So invisible when we would like (Oh, so much!) to see it with our natural eyes, yet so much evidence of it within, so much evidence of it beyond, if we but so control ourselves that we are willing to see it, know it, and feel it, and if we will but become so purified that we desire (if need be) to make some sacrifice,— sacrifices of pleasure, money and ambitions, if by and through any such sacrifices we can and will any more truly overcome, can and will any more truly benefit!

### The Life Beyond.

O mystery of mysteries!
O life beyond the goal!
Transcendent, everlasting;
The pure life of the soul.

### Religious Evolution.

It is natural for us to become divine. What a mistake it is to believe that divinity is, at all, an unnatural result of our earthly lives, or that the conditions of such divinity are given to us, from outside, rather than developed in us!

I believe in an evolutionary religion and in a religious evolution. That is to say, I believe in a religion which is gradually to be worked out, *per se*, and that all these things in and about us—the natural, the material, and the spiritual—are destined to evolve a truer, purer, higher life beyond.

Not necessarily beyond this world, but in and through what we call "the world," in a wide sense of the words, let each of us work out that which is above, gradually discarding and omitting the lower and lesser, and apprehending, instead, the greater and grander of the influences continually within our control. (Yet not "apprehending" them for our own gain, but rather in order to diffuse them, as possible, unto others.)

### *Upward.*

Draw the lines a little tighter,
   Spirit mine!
Make the life a little brighter,
   Spirit mine!
For the truth's sake be a fighter,
Show the world life may be whiter,
Purer, stronger, dearer, lighter,
   More divine!

If one wills, life may be higher,
   Spirit mine!
If one loves, God will be nigher,
   Spirit mine!
His affection does not tire,

Let us then His truth desire,
Seeking it past water, fire,
Gold and wine!

*Questions as to God.*

Questions as to God are questions as to the main fact of the universe.

It makes, indeed, all the difference in the world as to whether this life is, after all, a comparatively short one, and, following it, we enter upon an eternity of enjoyment; or, on the other hand, whether this life is, instead, our only one, and, following it, we enter upon an eternity of nothingness, going to be "a brother to the insensible rock" (as Bryant puts it), going to be "earth to earth," "ashes to ashes."

Why are we so blind and indifferent as to the spiritual side of our natures? Why do we so forget and overlook the fact that man is of a dual character,—the body which perishes, and the spirit which abides?

"God is spirit: and they that worship Him must worship in spirit and in truth?"

"Where got the man his confidence, except from truth? And what should the truth be, but God?"

"And if God thunder by law, the thunder is still His voice."

*Faith and Reason.*

Yet I know that God, in His infinite Wisdom, may allow some of His followers (possibly me, also), to lose their heads, to lose their grip and even their powers for good. We cannot reject facts. No matter how much we may wish to believe otherwise, we must accept facts as facts. Here is where faith transcends reason! Reason alone cannot satisfy us. It goes part way, it convinces us of truth, but reason is limited by the evidences of this life. Faith accepts the deductions of reason, but also envelops them with a belief in a past and a future which are beyond the grasp of mere reason. Reason says: "If man disobey natural law he must suffer the consequence." Faith sadly agrees: "Yes, surely, in this life, but beyond this life many will live differently, and those who have striven faithfully will be forgiven." Is not this sufficient to lead us to believe until death, no matter what the apparent side of our lives may become?

*"Heathenism" and Church-Attendance.*

The New England churches hold too strictly to the doctrine of "Christ alone, the only hope of salvation," and to belief in the Bible as "a perfect rule of faith and practice."

We of to-day, many of us, have learned the truth that a God-life may be lived just as well outside the churches as in them. We have learned, also, that "the Bible is only one of God's primers," by and through which He has taught and is teaching many wonderful truths, yet there is much necessary truth to be learned outside the Bible before we can to any degree realize, in ourselves and among the people we live with, that ideal life so held up to us in the Bible.

Modern Christianity has great problems and wonderful opportunities before it, and it will never solve these problems satisfactorily, nor make right use of its opportunities, until it broadens out its application of Christ's charity, until it awakes to the fact that "time makes ancient good uncouth," and until it has in its pulpits men of more fire, men of more sincere, intelligent and practical application of God's truths. Then we may expect to see one sort of "heathenism" lessened, but until that day the amount of church-attendance by earnest, thinking, sincere people, as well as by the careless, will not be increased.

## *To be a Christian.*

Is it to pray in word,
    And to accept a creed?
Often is prayer unheard,
    Christ seems to give no heed.

Live thou the Christian *life*,
  Seeking to know the best;
Patient and pure in strife,
  Then God will give thee rest.

*Without God.*

Is not this the condition toward which some of us are developing, to-day?

Yet I do not wish to be misunderstood, in asking this question. When I say "without God," I do not mean, "without God and without hope in the world." No such lifeless position as this, but rather a position and condition where there is not that "personal leading" of which we have often thought, in the past, in which we have been taught to believe, and for which we have often prayed and striven!

We ask this question, some of us, in all seriousness, not as atheists, not as infidels, but as those who have sought a personal God, only to find, instead, an influence, an essence, the good, but no personality which we can apprehend. We have discovered something of the truth as to the altruistic life, the spirit life, the man-life and the God-life, superior to the grosser, the more brutal, the more selfish life which many lead, but beyond this higher life we find, as yet, no evidence of any heavenly messengers, ready to protect the good and thwart the evil, in the world.

What then? Does this discovery lessen, in any way, our responsibility to others? Does it not, instead, intensify it, for if God were God would He not force men to do his will, if need be? On the other hand, if man be all to whom we may look for help, how important that each bear his part, lest our race, having lost, to a considerable extent, its belief in a personal God, sink back toward savagery.

How else can we explain many nineteenth-century crimes, except through loss of belief in God, and love of near-at-hand personal gain, regardless of truth and the rights of others?

At this time, therefore, what double need of every man being a man, one who will stand for the truth, the truth of a higher life, the truth of altruism, the truth of public benefit! Although we hardly realize it, we are in war-times, in times when the forces of evil are more aggressive than when they were held in check by a more national fear of God. Read almost any daily paper, with its record of frauds, embezzlements, murder, robberies and rapine. Who is to protect the widow, the orphan, the unsuspecting, the innocent, the guileless? One way is surely open. It is by man, for man. That, to-day, is our chief hope of salvation, yet how superficially do most of us realize this, when we think of it at all!

### *Fear.*

There is nothing to be afraid of except that remorse and deep regret which come to one if he discovers, at any time, that his life has been, in the main, toward evil rather than good, toward injuring rather than helping others; toward cheapening, debasing or in any way lowering the true standards of life; or toward making life itself of less value, dignity, and nobility, instead of adding to it that amount of benefit which we are able to see as possible, in our clearer moments; and which can gradually be apprehended and made effective, if we choose resolutely never to abide in or yield to our darker "visions."

*Unhappiness.*

There are no circumstances of life which can compel unhappiness. Circumstances may produce in us great suffering, great exertion, or great exhaustion, but there is a vast difference between these things and unhappiness. It is our privilege to so take suffering as to make happiness. Within ourselves, and within our control, are endless sources of delight. As we discover them, let us use these delights of memory, music of spirit, imagination and hope, so that they expand in us to the gradual subordination of disagreeable circumstances, to such an extent that we live superior to all disappointments!

### *The Sickness of Overwork.*

If one is ever losing his grip, because of overwork in the field of thought, give him rest, comfort and peacefulness, in proportion to his overwork, and you may restore him. If you are unable to do so, if his mind continues lacking in completeness to an alarming extent, comfort yourself with the thought that even insanity is not such a terrible thing as it sometimes appears to be; and suicide may be right or wrong. The objects in view make the difference.

God sees not as we see! Our part is only to use as well as we can those talents which are ours, without repining, and trust God for the rest.

### *Self-Help.*

Pardon me! I do what I think will be best.
Pardon me! But for me there now is no rest.

Pardon me! But whether life conquers or fails,
Unto the end, truly, self-help avails.

### *To Benefit.*

Be willing to be misunderstood;
If only, thereby, you effect the good.
Seek not alone your happiness to keep;
Truth must be won for others, ere you sleep.

### *Progress O'er the Sands.*

Ever lifting, ever sifting;
But with purpose; never drifting!

Lifting in the sense of "seeking to add to the stores of truth, and diminish the mountains of error." Sifting in the sense that, "Questioning sifts out the truth." Keeping in mind, also, the words,

"Part of thy manhood is to doubt and solve,
And rise to higher things."

### *As to Completed Results.*

God only can know;
Time only can show.

*Strength, Simplicity; Truth, Purity.*

Be strong, simple, true and pure! Not strong in any physical sense alone, although physical strength is something to be cultivated. Not simple in the way of being unintelligent, not true as to facts only, not pure in the sense of prudish; but better, broader, higher than either of these!

Be strong in the strength of a man, in its higher as well as in its lower meaning. Be strong in manliness!

Be simple in the way in which Lowell uses the word, in his *Commemoration Ode*,

> "Still patient in his simple faith sublime,
> Till the wise years decide."

Be true to thine own self, that is to thy best self, to the real revelation of truth in you, as you come to recognize and understand it.

Be pure in the sense of resolving and living as indicated by the poem:

"I will go forth 'mong men, not mailed in scorn
But in the armor of a pure intent.
And whether crowned or crownless when I fall
It matters not, so as God's work is done."

*The Spirit Life; What is it?*

It is the higher, larger, nobler life, within the control and suited to the needs of each one of us.

It is the man-life and the God-life, superior to the lower, lesser, and grosser life which we find all around us, and to which we are often inclined.

It is the power for good in human lives which enables them to overcome the temptation to make personal ends of these material things such as money, fame, honors and position, instead of using them as means for the benefit of others.

It is that influence which will, ere long, effect in our own country that result prophesied by Annie Besant when she said, in substance: "It shall come when each thinks for others and forgets self; when the general good is the recognized aim of the individual; when each outstretched hand is put forth for service, not for gain; then, when the brotherly act is the natural fruitage of the brotherly spirit, the republic of man will be born."

### *The Goodness of God.*

One might as well try to get away from moisture, and live without it, as to try to get away from the goodness of God. Does one get away from the moisture by leaving the ocean itself and climbing a mountain? Is not moisture drawn from the ocean by the sun, carried in clouds, and deposited even on mountain-peaks?

Read the following, and see if Sarah Wolsey has not put much truth into her poem, in saying:

"Sitting some day in a deeper mist,
    Silent, alone, some other day,
    An unknown bark, from an unknown bay,
By unknown waters lapped and kissed
    Shall near me through the spray.

"No flap of sail, no scraping of keel,
    Shadowy, dim, with a banner dark
    It will hover, will pause, and I shall feel
A hand that leads me, and quietly steal
    To the cold strand, and embark.

"Embark for that far, mysterious realm
    Where the fathomless, trackless waters flow.
    I shall feel a Presence dim, and know
Thy hand, dear Lord, upon the helm,
    Nor be afraid to go!"

*A Writer's Life.*

Whatever he may find, 'tis less than he has sought;
Whatever he may give, 'tis all too poorly wrought;

Whatever he may speak, 'tis less than he
    has thought;
Whatever he may teach, 'tis less than he
    was taught.

### *Content.*

To-night, thank God! I am content
No matter when the call is sent,
No matter when my soul is blent
    With other souls, above.

Contented here, and perfect there;
Never was promise half so fair
As that which tells us, "God does care;
    His words are words of love."

Although the day may still seem long,
And though your life is full of wrong;
Through evil and through good, be strong,
    Be patient and be brave.

God's messengers may be named, "Pain,"
"Sorrow," "Trial,"—yet not in vain
These messengers all sing one strain,
    "Remember, He will save."

## Essays and Poems

### Literal Christianity.

Christianity, as we ordinarily understand the word, is, I believe, a beautiful, noble and touching effort to personify that which has not personality. It is an effort conceived and carried out, expressed and carried on, in the main, by noble men who believe it to be the best way of expressing truth to others, men who, themselves, believe to a great extent in that which they teach, yet few of them dare assert that they are "led by Christ"; because they lack that personal leading which alone can warrant such an assertion.

We of to-day, many of us, no longer believe in "Christianity" in any such literal sense as we used to do.

### What is the Soul?

It is the vital, eternal and transcendent part of us, that part which (as Wordsworth says) :

—" rises with us, our life's star,—
Not in entire forgetfulness,

And not in utter nakedness,
But trailing clouds of glory do we come
From God, who is our home:"

Does this "we," as used by him, here, refer to the earthly, physical or selfish self which is so apparent, most of the time, in this world? Not at all, but rather to that higher self which is often so hidden as to be scarcely discernible for a time, yet which always leads us away from and beyond the lesser things of this life which continually tempt us, which assure us of its truth, its reality, and its eternity of life, which rebukes us whenever we turn to lower satisfactions, and which proves itself stronger than any temptation to doubt, to fear, or to lasting discouragement.

*Earth's Message.*

" Wearied and worn by the struggle here,
  Bruised and torn by the ceaseless strife,
What is the message of earth, my dear?
  What is the meaning of death, of life?"

"Death's meaning, often, is but *more life*,
  Glories that soften, year after year;
Peace, joy, and happiness, freedom from strife,
That is the message of earth, my dear!"

### *Afterward.*

Shall I, as some tell me: "Go in for wealth;
Bury your feelings; consider your health:
  Forget her?" "Forget *her?*" I answer, "Oh, no!
Life may in many ways seem but a show,
Full of appearances,—yet in my heart
Still lives a vision which nothing can part,
  Nothing can sever and naught take away,
  There it remains to the close of life's day."

And when, beyond this world, "life's work well done,"
I shall have passed from the sight of earth's sun,
  Will I then think of her? Will I be near?

If she should question me, would I then hear?
Yes! 'neath the law of God, if we still live
In such a manner as answer to give
To those who need us, to those who desire
Only God's music, to fit to life's lyre.

### *To Rev. John Hutchins.*

January 1, 1896.

(A NEW YEAR'S GREETING TO A NEW PASTOR.)

Welcome to our Litchfield hills
Him who with God's Presence thrills,—
  We, indeed, do welcome you,
  May you be both brave and true,
Lead the people through the night,
Lead the people to the Light,
  Speak the words of right and truth
  To the children and the youth,
Preach throughout the coming year
With a heart that knows no fear,
  Blest beyond all with God's love
  Given from His home above!

## *Two Pictures.*

First—Coming down on the car this morning, and referring to the rain which had been falling in sheets since three o'clock, one man said: "I found a tramp standing under the eaves of my barn a few minutes ago, dripping wet, thin and sickly, using what little shelter he could find. He told me that he had been there all night. He had a bad cold, too. It's a hard life, is n't it?"

Second—Going into the Public Library this afternoon, to glance at the last issue of *Harper's Weekly*, I found as its frontispiece the design accepted for a Cathedral to be erected at Washington by the Episcopalians, to cost three million dollars.

One picture is an isolated instance of an extreme of poverty. The other is a very striking case of rich and self-glorifying religious pride and sectarian interest,

Both are part of that " world " into which the Saviour sent his disciples, saying to them :

"Provide neither gold, nor silver, nor brass in your purses, nor scrip for your journey," saying to them, at another time: "Inasmuch as ye have done it unto one of the least of these, my brethren, ye have done it unto Me," and telling them also, that "The Son of Man hath not where to lay his head."

Yet one division of His modern disciples need a three million dollar cathedral in which to listen to the words of the head of their denomination in America, and "the least of these," although still called "brethren," must yet remain in rags, in dampness, and in a state of sickness.

Why? Because "unworthy"? Perhaps so. Very likely so, in this particular case! But is it not true that many a man and many a woman, honest, hard-working, and God-fearing, is having too hard a struggle amid the "hard-times" near the close of this nineteenth century, to justify any church in putting three million dollars into a grand cathedral, rather than into "daily bread" ("bread of life," most truly!) for the suffering ones?

We are Christian in our theory, Christian in our philosophy; but when it comes to our actual practice, are not most of us, in our churches and in our services, self-glorifying in effect, rather than broadly charitable?

Santa Barbara, Cal., January 27, 1896.

### *How to Live.*

Live as thou wouldst live when thy soul is clear!
Live as the birds live when clouds disappear!
Live as the saints live when their Home is near!
      Then wilt thou die in peace.

### *A Conqueror.*

  He kept up the standards
    Through thick and through thin;
  He loved not the evil,
    He loved not the sin.

### What is Sin?

Sin is the being untrue to that within our control which is best. Sin is a choosing of the lesser and lower, rather than the greater, the nobler, the higher. Sin is a loving of evil, rather than good. Sin is not so much a matter of our apparent actions (although they, of course, are the visible fruit of our thoughts, and must be that by which others judge us). Rather, "to him that thinketh anything to be sin, to him it is sin." "As a man thinketh, so is he."

"Every man according to the light he has," yet in matters of law we must not judge too delicately on the question of a man's "light." The good of the community should be considered, the need of making an example!

What is better than the sacrifice of the individual *for the public good?*

### A Prayer.

God keep me from insanity!
God keep me from profanity

And cruel inhumanity!
Amen.

## A Statement.

At the risk of being misunderstood, I make the following statement:

I believe that to continue to help this struggling world, after death, to use our superior powers, at that time, for the benefit of those yet on earth, would be a better life than to use a harp among the redeemed, in singing praises!

## An Answer to "Isolation of Individuality."

In the *Los Angeles Times*, last January, G. W. Robertson published an essay, "The Isolation of Individuality." The extreme loneliness of soul described by him may be true in some particulars, and undoubtedly is, but it seemed as though the thought was left in incomplete and depressing shape, for the essay did not give the results gathered by most of the really lonely characters of history, and the effect of their loneliness upon their work, and upon those who learn of it afterward.

Let me illustrate the truth which I wish to make clear. Would Dante ever have written as he did, if he had not been lonely? Would Longfellow have written either *The Bridge* or *The Light of Stars* if he had not been very lonely? And is it true that these two great souls, through their writing, touch other souls only at one or two points?

Mr. Robertson says: "No soul touches another soul except at one or two points, and those chiefly external." On the other hand, listen for a moment to Emerson, when he says: "A soul living from a great depth of being awakens in us, by its actions and words, by its very looks and manners, the same power and beauty that a gallery of sculpture or of pictures is wont to animate." Are there no altruistic compensations in such soul-loneliness as that referred to in "Isolation of Individuality"? Surely there are, and we regret that they were not pictured by Mr. Robertson himself, in direct connection with the loneliness he describes, —loneliness which is, at times, almost unbearable, were it not for the thought which continually comes to us, the thought that real loneliness is by no means in vain.

*Evil is but Perverted Good.*

I have one theory which came to me with striking force, years ago. I entered it at that time in my note-book, and have become more and more convinced of its truth since then. It is simply that evil is but perverted good.

What else can we believe, if we believe at all as Mr. Whittier did, as expressed in his words,

" All is of God that is, and is to be;
And God is good " ?

Who, then, is to blame for the fact that the good ("the God in you") is so often perverted? Not angels and not devils, certainly, but men! There is the answer to many such questions, and the solution of many problems. In men!

Yet, alas! how often do we look for outside reasons, instead of placing the blame where it belongs—*i. e.*, upon and through our own selves and *our* "adjustment."

*PART II.*

QUOTATIONS AND SUGGESTIONS.

# QUOTATIONS AND SUGGESTIONS.

*The True Man.*

Take thou no thought for aught save right and truth.
Life holds for finer souls no equal judge;
Honors and wealth are baubles to the wise,
And pleasure flies on swifter wing than youth
If in thy heart thou bearest seeds of hell.
Though all men smile, get what shall be thy gain;
Though all men frown, of truth and right remain;
Take thou no thought for self, for all is well.
LEWIS MORRIS.

"The sum of wisdom is, that the time is never lost that is devoted to work."
EMERSON.

"Rightly to be is the sole inlet of rightly to know." *Ibid.*

"The only true knowledge is that conscious knowledge which speaks out of the soul."

Dr. A. C. Hirst.

"The Parnassan heights that lie up yonder, bathed with sun-glow, are reached by the man and not by the mob."

L. E. Mosher.

Matthew Arnold has said that, "What distinguishes the greatest poets is their powerful and profound application of ideas to life."

*An Ideal Popular Leader.*

He is one who counts no public toil so hard
   As idly glittering pleasures; one controlled
By no mob's haste, nor swayed by gods of
   gold;

Prizing, not courting, all just men's regard;
With none but manhood's ancient order
    starred,
  Nor crowned with titles less august and
    old
Than human greatness; large brained, limpid
    souled ;
  Whom dreams can hurry not, nor doubts
    retard ;
Born, nurtured of the people ; living still
  The people's life ; and though their noblest
    flower,
In naught removed from them save alone
  In loftier virtue, wisdom, courage, power ;
The ampler vision, the serener will,
  And the fixed mind, to no light dallyings
    prone.
WILLIAM WATSON.

### *The Greatest of All.*

He only is great of heart who floods the world with a great affection. He only is great of mind who stirs the world with great thoughts. He only is great of will who does something to shape the world to a great career, and he is greatest who does the most of all these things and does them best.

R. D. HITCHCOCK.

"We cannot act without a theory of life; and to whom shall we look for such a theory, except to those who, undaunted by the difficulties of the task, ask once more, and strive to answer, those questions which man cannot entirely escape, as long as he continues to think and act?"

"Browning as a Philosopher and<br>Religious Teacher."

"But you have reached many people with your poems, and helped many," I suggested; "there was always a heart-touch in them." "There was a heart-need in them, I doubt not," he said, with tears in his eyes, "for my life has been very incomplete, sometimes very lonely."

WHITTIER.

# Quotations and Suggestions

" Though his life was filled with bitter and crushing disappointments, we may search his writings in vain for any word which can be made to indicate a doubt as to the principles which guided his actions or as to the result of his work."

>Written of Paul, in Mr. Symington's Sermon, of January 18, 1885.

After all, I may write, and underline, and punctuate with great care, without giving to anyone quite the meaning that some special words and sentences have to me. Yet it seems as though others would gather something of that which I so much enjoy!

*To My Pen.*

Nay, not so fast! A mettled steed thou art.
   And swift to dash across the wide white plain!
But ere we on our morning's journey start
   Let us resolve some certain point to gain.

It boots not if we dip in old romance,
   Or weave a rhyme to lull a babe asleep,

Or sing the trifling pleasures of the dance,
  Or tell of happiness serene and deep.

But we must reach at eve the goal Content,
  By level or by labyrinthine way,
And feel the bygone hours were not ill spent
  Nor wasted, so we may now humbly say:

"A word there was with loving kindness
    fraught,
  A hint that might a drooping faith renew,
A plea for softer speech, for purer thought,
  A message hopeful or a warning true."

And were no man helped onward for a mile,
  No fainting brother lifted from the dust,
No wan face won a moment to a smile—
  "'T were better, pen, we should forever
    rust!"

JULIA DITTO YOUNG.

"Question not, but live and labor
   Till the goal be won,
 Helping every feeble neighbor

Seeking help from none;
Life is mostly froth and bubble,
Two things stand like stone—
Kindness in another's trouble,
Courage in your own!"

ADAM LINDSAY GORDON.

"—higher than this can no man attain 'to live to the level of his highest thought.'"

UNKNOWN.

"Is there a dream or a hope in you, that makes your life look richer and nobler? Lay your hand in that, just as you would into the open hand of God."

THOREAU.

"To trust is the greatest step God-wards that any soul can take."

T. T. MUNGER.

"Phillips, when he devoted his life to the Anti-Slavery cause, made a great sacrifice. He deliberately gave up all hope of wealth, social position, and political honor which his

birth and his splendid intellectual gifts justified him in looking forward to."
CARLOS MARTYN.

"This or that; not this and that."
PHILIP G. HAMERTON.

"He kept his honesty and truth,
  His independent tongue and pen,
And moved in manhood as in youth,
  Pride of his fellow-men."
"Burns," FITZ-GREENE HALLECK.

"He was Ishmael enough to know the value of liberty."
KIPLING.

Fill needs first, then wants.

"Greatness consists not in the abundance of our wants, but in the smallness of our needs."
UNKNOWN.

"I have very few wants," she answered brightly; "and wealth is only a relative word after all."
BEATRICE HARRADEN.

"All things lovely and righteous are possible for those who believe in their possibility, and who determine that for their part they will make every day's work contribute to them."

JOHN RUSKIN.

Notice, this does not say all things material, financial, or commercial, but "all things lovely and righteous"! The outside, the circumstances, the material,—these are but partly within our control, so although we may not and should not neglect them, we may and should look beyond them, and ever through them apprehend the blessings, the privileges and the duties which belong to those higher regions and elements which we call soul and mind and spirit, in contrast to the lesser powers of heart and brain and body.

"The happiness of your life depends upon the character of your thoughts."

MARCUS AURELIUS.

If we keep our minds occupied only with good thoughts, we will not be wearied by the sameness of our daily round.

> " Count me o'er earth's chosen heroes, they were men who stood alone
> While the men they agonized for hurled the contumelious stone ;
> Stood serene, and down the future saw the golden beam incline
> To the side of perfect justice, mastered by their faith sublime,
> By one man's plain truth to manhood and to God's supreme design."
>
> LOWELL.

After all, not more refining of fine-spun theories, but more refining of ourselves, and through ourselves "the world," to some extent, is what is most needed.

> " Patience and abnegation of self, and devotion to others,
> These were the lessons a life of trial and sorrow had taught her."
>
> *Evangeline,*

*De:* concerning; *votum:* giving—so devotion to others means a giving of that which concerns others, not perhaps a giving up, for that depends upon how others are best to be benefited.

" Impulsive, earnest, prompt to act,
 And make the generous thought a fact,
 Keeping with many a light disguise
 The secret of self-sacrifice."
UNKNOWN.

The secret and the true test of self-sacrifice is its unselfishness. Not its appearance, not necessarily its denial of self, but its motive. The appearance and the amount of self-denial are incidents, not causes.

" There is no sacrifice to those who love, in what is borne for the one we love."
*Last Days of Pompeii.*

" Why not take life with cheerful trust,
 With faith in the power of weakness?
 The slenderest daisy lifts its head

With courage, and in meekness.
>    A sunny face
>    Hath holy grace."
>                                    UNKNOWN.

Fly high! Fly high! It is better to aim at a star, and enjoy the light of constellations alone, than to creep along an ordinary plane in ordinary company. The poet must lead, and point above!

"Aim at the highest, and never mind the money."

Though aiming at the highest, put it in a sufficiently light way, so that it will attract.

"Blessed is the man who has found his work. Let him ask no other blessedness."
                                    CARLYLE.

*Keep Up the Standard!*

"Know Thyself."

"But what I truly believe I was meant to do, that will I do, no matter what it costs."
                                    MARY HALLOCK FOOTE.

*Clear Sight.*

I think 'tis time, yes! fully time to see!
To ask myself (this other self, whate'er it be)
What, of these influences, belongs to me?

J. O. C.

—" The intense Dante is intense in all things."

Thomas Carlyle.

" By labor and intent study, which I take to be my portion in life, I may haply leave something so written to after times that they will not willingly let it die."

John Milton.

" The talent of success is nothing more than doing what you can do, well, without a thought of fame."

Longfellow.

"To me it seems incomparably better that any one's accidental moods should be haunted by a subtle or noble thought, or by a line that has soul or music in it, than for one to be a master of learning."

E. T. McLaughlin.

"All one's life is music, if one but uses the stops rightly, and in time."

MENDELSSOHN.

"Not by his money, or his power,
Not by his intellect, indeed;
Not by the pleasure of an hour,
Nor by the wording of his creed,
But by the strong will,
But by the soul's grace,
But by the yearnings which thread
Night and day,
Soft and still,
Till they glow in his face,
Do we tell man's life
Forever and aye."

UNKNOWN.

"What a man is engraves itself on his face, on his form, on his fortunes, in letters of light which all may read but himself."

EMERSON.

Like that which a man thinks most of, does he become. The thoughts of a man's heart and soul are those which really affect us. Yes, and affect him, just as surely as the currents of electricity affect the carbons in electric lights! They make him glow with health, with love, with pure light, or they consume him with the flames of fever, hate and passion.

Not that the thoughts are everything! There are, indeed, natural causes for health, for affection, for anger, for hate, but how important it is to think as we should, during these times of special trial or excitement, during the temptation to wild, wicked, or injudicious actions, for it is just this that makes the difference between heroes and criminals.

Carlyle says: "The thoughts they had were the parents of the actions they did." And he goes further, saying: "Their feelings were parents of their thoughts; it was the unseen and spiritual in them which determined the outward and actual."

"We live in deeds, not years; in thoughts,
 not breaths;
In feelings, not in figures on a dial.
We should count time by heart-throbs. He
 most lives
Who thinks most, feels the noblest, acts
 the best.
Life's but a means unto an end, that end—
Beginning, mean and end to all things—
 God."
PHILIP JAMES BAILEY.

"Poets are all who love, who feel great
 truths
And tell them ; and the truth of truths is
 love."
BAILEY.

*New-England.*

Wherever thought is deep and strong,
Wherever conscience fights with wrong,
Wherever manhood dares to die,
And womanhood is pure and high;
On mountain peak or plain or sea
The soul's one cry must ever be:
 Thank God for old New-England.

The warrior's sword and poet's pen
Are thine to wield, but only when
The cause of right demands the blow,
When thou wouldst lay proud error low;
Then only does thy face of love
Grow dark with sternness from above,
   Oh, grandly great New-England!


For those enslaved in life, in thought,
Thy blood, thy tongue, hath freedom
   bought.
The arm of justice in its might,
The thrilling voice of truth and right,
The patriot ardor, glowing warm
With courage calm in battle storm,
   Are in thy name, New-England.
Lewis W. Smith.


"You will find life full of sweet savour, if you do not expect from it what it cannot give."
Renan.

"It is the little rift within the lute,
  That bye-and-bye will make the music mute,
And ever-widening slowly silence all."
                                        TENNYSON.

"He who is false to present duty, breaks a thread in the loom, and will find the flaw when he may have forgotten the cause."
                                        H. W. BEECHER.

"New occasions teach new duties.
  Time makes ancient good uncouth,—"

Not untrue, not valueless, but "uncouth," inapplicable, perhaps, to present needs, in the letter, although the noble spirit of the "ancient good" is and will continue to be a strong inspiration to many of us!

"The only conclusive evidence of a man's sincerity is that he gives himself for a principle. Words, money, all things else, are comparatively easy to give away, but when a man makes a gift of his daily life and practice it is plain that the truth, whatever it may be, has taken possession of him."

LOWELL.

"Man will ever wrestle; he will never trust."

GOETHE.

This is the same idea, as to "trust" as Longfellow uses, in saying: "Trust no future, howe'er pleasant," is it not? Yet Longfellow goes further, and more nearly completes the thought by adding,

"Let the dead past bury its dead.
Act, act in the living present,
Heart within and God o'erhead."

"In the reverent pause with which the heart answers these questions, the instinct and the habit of trust in our Creator are gently justified."

ELIZABETH STUART PHELPS.

"I'd just gently like bring her round some time; keep on prayin' an' all that, but don't force it."

MARGARET DELAND.

"Like a high soul, which feels itself so great
It can with an untroubled courage wait
Hour and event, which surely come at last,
Since, in God's certain order, none is overpast."

UNKNOWN.


"Strong sense, deep feeling, passions strong,
A hate of tyrant and of knave,
A love of right, a scorn of wrong,
Of coward and of slave,—

"A kind, true heart, a spirit high,
That could not fear and would not bow,
Were written in his manly eye
And on his manly brow."

FITZ-GREENE HALLECK.


—"He was passionately absorbed in forming ideas on the great questions of life and its relations."

*Life of Napoleon*, by IDA M. TARBELL.

"The nation is now the paramount object," he wrote; "my natural inclinations are now in harmony with my duties."
*Ibid.*

"He had won his place as any poor and ambitious boy in any country and in any age must win his—by hard work, by grasping at every opportunity, by constant self-denial, by courage in every failure, by springing to his feet after every fall."
*Ibid.*

"Of all paths a man could strike into, there is, at any given moment a best path for every man; a thing which, here and now, it were of all things wisest for him to do, which, would he but be led or driven to do, he were then doing 'like a man,' as we phrase it. This path, to find this path and walk in it, is the one thing needful for him."
CARLYLE.

"No one lives his own life who does not dwell in his higher rather than in his lower

faculties. To grow toward the ideal, to realize the heavenly image that we shall bear even as we have borne the image of the earthly—this is living one's own life."
UNKNOWN.

"It is said by a recent writer—that Jesus Christ taught no new doctrine. Perhaps not, but he made real and vital an old doctrine."
DR. LYMAN ABBOTT.

"Make God real, make art holy, make righteousness beautiful, and the family tie universal."
G. W. CABLE.

"The purer life draws nigher,
  Every year;
And its morning star climbs higher,
  Every year;
Earth's hold on us grows slighter,
The heavy burdens lighter,
And the dawn immortal brighter,
  Every year!"
ALBERT PIKE.

"Build thee more stately mansions, O my soul,
As the swift seasons roll!
Leave thy low-vaulted past!
Let each new temple, nobler than the last,
Shut thee from heaven with a dome more vast,
Till thou at length art free,
Leaving thine outgrown shell by life's unresting sea!"
OLIVER WENDELL HOLMES.

"The material part of us ought to keep growing thinner to let the soul out when its time comes, and the soul ought to keep growing bigger and stronger every day, until it bursts the body at length, as a growing nut does its shell."
GEORGE MACDONALD.

"Mr. Gladstone is a believer in the theory that a man can do better mental work every year to extreme old age if he takes care of his body. He claims that the mind grows stronger and clearer as the body loses vitality, and that it is only disease of the latter that can prevent an intellectual progress that will go on to the end. He is certainly a good illustration of his working theory."

UNKNOWN.

—" The head and face were those of a man who might move the world more readily than the world could move him—a man to be twice twelve times tortured into the shapeless cripple he was, without a groan, much less a confession; a man to yield his life but never a purpose or a point; a man born in armor, and assailable only through his loves."

*Re* "Simonides," *Ben-Hur*, p. 183.

How these illustrate the truth that every higher man must (if he would continue "upward") continually keep the body under, and bring all appetites into subjection, rather than allow any to become master!

"Here then we have the first important condition of any real, true success in life, the conviction that the circumstances of a man's

life are never more clearly a part of God's plan for that man than when they seem to leave him no alternative. There is no belief so inspiriting and comforting as that all these things, the patient struggle with adversity, the daily toil, no matter what, are, under God, preparing and perfecting us."
REV. CHARLES SYMINGTON.

"The tissue of the life to be
   We weave with colors all our own,
And in the field of destiny
   We reap as we have sown."
WHITTIER.

May not "the life to be" just as well and truly refer to life from henceforth, in this world, as well as to the life beyond? Is it not always true that "Life is as we take it," rather than as it appears to be, on the surface, and does not the world become what each of us helps to make it, for better or worse? And according to the lights of our lives, be they greater or smaller, let them be directed toward and for the right, the true, and the good, in and through both local and general circumstance, rather than ever downward or backward!

" Walk in the light;
   So shalt thou know
  Thy path, though thorny, bright!
  For God by faith shall dwell in thee;
And God himself is Light."

If I were only a little freer and stronger, physically, just at present, I would begin an essay or composition of some sort to be called "Finding the God in our Circumstances," an elaboration of the tenet in *One Man's Thesis*, which says, "God is an essence." How much of my writing needs a little more elaboration! If I but had more money, more freedom from pain and less "head-trouble," how clearly could I define some of the truths which, in spite of these disadvantages, I have already partly expressed! God only knows the whys and wherefores of the often fruitless thoughts and "inspirations" which have so continually come to me with such power that to attempt to evade them was almost useless, no matter how much some temporary reason might appeal to me as adverse to them.

At times there has been some fruit, surely, and I've no desire to belittle that, but the fact is often apparent that I have suffered more than most men, and have reaped little as an offset to that suffering, in the way of any sufficient compensation, *per se*, to any persons (except certain friends, to whom it does seem as though the same amount of benefit might as well have been given at less cost, if I had only been allowed to work out the lesser plans toward which I have continually held.)

> "Yet nerve thy spirit to the proof,
> And blench not from thy chosen lot."
> BRYANT.

Mr. Symington truly said: "As he looks, wearied perhaps with toil, the temptation comes to shirk. He sees only the contrast, then—there comes to him the remembrance that his lot is chosen and his work divinely appointed. This thought becomes an element of strength."

"The New Brotherhood still exists and grows. There are many who imagined that as it had been raised out of the earth by Elsmere's genius, so it would sink with him. Not so! He would have fought the struggle to victory with surpassing force, with a brilliancy and rapidity none after him could rival. But the struggle was not his. His effort was but a fraction of the effort of the race. In that effort, and in the Divine force behind it, is our trust, as was his."

Mrs. Humphrey Ward.

"Have we not all one Father? Has not He created us all? Why should we be bigoted and not love our neighbors as ourselves? Death makes us all equals. There are about one thousand different religions on this earth and but *one* in the hereafter."

Rabbi Ben Akiba.

"Work for the union of all who love, in the service of those who suffer!"

W. T. STEAD.

"Blessed is the memory of those who have kept themselves unspotted *from* the world! Yet more blessed the memory of those who kept themselves unspotted *in* the world."

MRS. JAMESON.

"So to the calmly gathered thought
  The innermost of life is taught,
  The mystery, dimly understood,
  That love of God is love of good;
  That to be saved is only this,—
  Salvation from our selfishness."

J. G. WHITTIER.

"I praise him not; it were too late;
  And some innative weakness there must be
  In him who condescends to victory
  Such as the Present gives, and cannot wait,
    Safe in himself as in a fate.
    So always firmly he;
    He knew to bide his time,

And can his fame abide,
Still patient in his simple faith sublime,
Till the wise years decide."

J. R. LOWELL.

*The Shadow Chaser.*

With outstretched hands he saw his child-joys flee,
And vanish with the passing of the day,
Like ships that hold their course far out at sea
Nor heed the anxious watchers in the bay.
And glad youth found him following, ardent-eyed,
The fleeting phantoms that he ever lost;
And all his eager manhood seemed denied
The sweet reward such weary searching cost.
Then came, at length, life's lord, sweet Death, and to him said:
"Oh! loyal heart, well done, behold thy wage!"
And lo! with fadeless beauty overspread,

The shadow of his childhood, youth and age."

HELEN GRAY CONE.

Might she not more suitably have used a word calling Death a messenger, rather than "lord"? Yet in all the other words, how true this poem is!

*The Agnostic's Question—" Is Life Worth Living?"*

Life is a thing worth living to the brave,
    Who fear not fortune's spite; in truth who trust.
Whose spirit, not thralled by pride or earthward lust,
    Stands up, while mortal tumults round them rave,
Like Teneriffe above the ocean wave;
    Who mailed in duty, with divine disgust
Recoil from frivolous joys and aims unjust,
    Nor miss rewards which Reason scorns to crave.

Life is worth living to those souls of light
  Who live for others, and by gift bestow
On them the jubilant beams their own by right,
  Who knowing life's defects, more inly know
This life is not the Temple, but the Gate
  Where men, secure of entrance, watch and wait.

AUBREY DE VERE.

"Moreover, seeing as God giveth me to now, the ends I dream of are to be wrought by fair means alone."

*Ben-Hur.*

### *Mirage.*

Treasure the shadow. Somewhere, firmly based,
  Arise those turrets that in cloud-land shine;
Somewhere to thirsty toilers of the waste
  Yon phantom well-spring is a living sign.

Treasure the shadow. Somewhere past thy
  sight,
    Past all men's sight, waits the true heaven
    at last;
Tell them whose fear would put thy hope
  to flight,
    There are no shadows save from substance
    cast.
                        EDITH M. THOMAS.


### *What Doth It Matter?*

It matters not the manner of our going
  Sooner or later comes the Master's call;
In summer's sunshine or in winter's blowing
  The message comes to all.

Perchance our last farewell we may be taking
  In calm communion with a loving heart,
Or in fierce winds or sudden waves high
  breaking
  Our spirits may depart.

It matters not, if only we are ready,
  Doing His will, accepted by His grace,

Bearing the banner of His great love steady,
    And standing in our place.

It matters not the way of life's conclusion,
    None knoweth how God's message then
        shall come,
In calmest hush or wildest storm's confusion,
    He will but bear us home.

L. C. WOOD.

### *The Prospect.*

Methinks we do as fretful children do,
    Leaning their faces on a window pane
    To sigh the glass dim with their own
        breath's stain,
And shut the sky and landscape from their
        view;
And thus, alas! since God the Maker drew
    A mystic separation 'twixt those twain,
    The life beyond us and our souls in pain,
We miss the prospect which we are called
        unto
    By grief we are fools to use. Be still and
        strong,

O man, my brother! hold thy sobbing breath,
  And keep thy soul's large window pure
    from wrong,
That so, as life's appointment issueth,
  Thy vision may be clear to watch along
The sunset consummation lights of death.
        ELIZABETH BARRETT BROWNING.

> " Life's work well done,
> Life's race well run,
> Life's crown well won,
> Then comes rest."

Not on the road, not in the race, itself, but afterward! We may enjoy partial and temporary rests, halts and refreshings, here, but, "the rest which remaineth" comes later than the present.

### *A Morning Thought.*

What if some morning when the stars were
  paling,
  And the dawn whitened, and the east was
    clear,

Strange peace and rest fell on me from the presence
  Of a benignant spirit standing near:

And I should tell him, as he stood beside me,
  "This is our earth—most friendly earth, and fair;
Daily its sea and shore through sun and shadow
  Faithful it turns, robed in its azure air.

"There is blest living here, loving and serving,
  And quest of truth and serene friendships dear;
But stay not, Spirit! Earth has one destroyer—
  His name is Death; flee, lest he find thee here!"

And what if then, while the still morning brightened,
  And freshened in the elm the Summer's breath,

Should gravely smile on me the gentle angel,
And take my hand and say, "My name is Death."
EDGAR ROWLAND SILL.

### *The Day's Work.*

Do thy day's work, my dear,
Though fast and dark the clouds are drifting near,
Though time has little left for hope and very much for fear.

Do thy day's work, though now
The hand must falter and the head must bow,
And far above the falling foot shows the bold mountain brow.

Yet there is left us,
Who on the valley's verge stand waiting thus,
A light that lies far in the west,—soft, faint, but luminous.

We can give kindly speech,
And ready helping hands to all and each,
And patience to the watchful ones, by smiling silence teach.

We can give gentle thought,
And charity, by life's long lesson taught,
And wisdom, from old faults lived down, by toil and failure wrought.

We can give love unmarred
By selfish snatch of happiness, unjarred
By the keen arms of power or joy that make youth cold and hard.

And if gay hearts reject
The gifts we hold—would fain fare unchecked
On the bright road that scarce yields all that eager eyes expect,

Why, do thy day's work still;
The calm, deep founts of love are slow to chill,

And heaven may yet the harvest yield, the
workworn hands to fill.
Chicago *Herald*.

"I read it on the brow of night,
   Before the dawn bursts on the sky,
   The darker hour, the deeper sigh,
Are tokens of some softer light.

"The lurking vice, the tainting shame,
   The ills of earth, with all its moans,
   May be hewn into stepping-stones
To climb the golden hill of fame."
Part of *Stepping Stones*,<br>a poem by W. A. HAVENER.

"Upon your hearts it is written. Take it down to them."
OLIVE SCHREINER'S *Dreams*.

"There is a kingdom on the earth, though it is not of it—a kingdom of wider bounds than the earth. Its existence is a fact as our hearts are facts, and we journey through it from birth to death without seeing it;

nor shall any man see it until he hath first known his own soul; for the kingdom is not for him, but for his soul."
*Ben-Hur.*

Those things which we never see, literally, this side of the "transition," but which we always feel! They are,

—" an enigma to all who do not or cannot understand that every man is two in one—a deathless Soul and a mortal Body.

"On the earth, yet not of it—not for men, but for their souls—a dominion, nevertheless, of unimaginable glory."
*Ben-Hur.*

—"He became subject unto the law of death." Yes! But was He not, indeed, superior to death, and may not we become so, too, rather than think of and meet Death as "the king of terrors," or anything by which we, ourselves, are ever to be conquered?

"If such a one, having so much to give,
Gave all, laying it down for love of men,
And thenceforth spent himself to search for truth.—
Surely, at last, far off, sometime, somewhere,
The veil would lift for his deep-searching eyes,
The road would open for his painful feet,
That should be won for which he lost the world,
And Death might find him conqueror of death."
*Light of Asia.*

"'I see the vision of a poor, weak soul striving after good. It was not cut short; and in the end, it learned, through tears and much pain, that holiness is an infinite compassion for others; that greatness is to take the common things of life and walk truly among them; that happiness is a great love and much serving. It was not cut short; and it loved what it had learned,—it loved— and——'

"Was that all she saw in the corner?"
*The Story of an African Farm.*

—" Saw within
A worthier image for the sanctuary,
And shaped it forth before the multitude,
Divinely human, raising worship so
To higher reverence more mixed with love."
GEORGE ELIOT.

—" The whole of the story is not written here, but it is suggested. And the attribute of all true art, the highest and the lowest, is this: that it says more than it says, and takes you away from itself. There is nothing so universally intelligible as truth. What your work wants is not truth, but beauty of external form, the other half of art."
*Story of an African Farm.*

" Bounded by themselves and unregardful
In what state God's other work may be,
Into their own tasks their powers outpouring,
These attain the mighty life you see."
MATTHEW ARNOLD.

# Quotations and Suggestions 87

"They talk of genius, it is nothing but this: that a man knows what he can do best, and does it, and nothing else."

"Taste everything a little, look at everything a little, but live for one thing."
*Story of an African Farm.*

Let that "one thing" be the establishment and application of real truth, in and through "the world"!

*The Secret of Success.*

Not fancy merely, or the rush
Of feeling, guides the pen or brush,
As tint by tint, and line by line,
The verses grow, the colors shine!
We find with these the crowning art,
Whose magic can alone impart
To genius all its highest gains—
The faculty of taking pains.

They learn the secret of success,
Who seek—content with nothing less—
Perfection, with no aim beside,

And, missing this, dissatisfied!
And they alone, in life's brief day,
To fame and honor win their way
Who first achieve, for such high gains,
The strenuous art of taking pains.
J. R. EASTWOOD, in *The Quiver*.

"The great thing in life is to be in earnest, say what you mean, not what you think you ought to say, and strive for the thing you want—not for the thing which the philosophy of the moment has made fashionable, or the emotion of a day has made a little tempting."
JOHN OLIVER HOBBES.

"Trifles, lighter than straws, are levers in the building of character."
UNKNOWN.

"By our errors we see deeper into life. They help us."

"'It was a small thing, but life is made up of small things, as a body is built up of cells. What has been done in small things, can be done in large. Shall be,' she said softly."
*Story of an African Farm.*

"He was so severe a lover of justice, and so precise a lover of truth, that he was superior to all possible temptations for the violation of either."
FLORENCE EARLE COATES
on MATTHEW ARNOLD.

"In him was that rare combination of qualities ascribed to Pericles—a genius the most fervid, with passions the best regulated."
*Ibid.*

"There is, I know not how, in the minds of men, a certain presage, as it were, of a future existence, and this takes the deepest root, and is most discoverable, in the greatest geniuses and the most exalted souls."
CICERO.

"The lifting up of the hands brings no salvation; redemption is from within; it is wrought out by the soul itself, with suffering and through time."
>*Story of an African Farm.*

"Our acts our angels are, or good or ill,
Our fatal shadows that walk by us still."
>BEAUMONT and FLETCHER.

"To believe your own thought, to believe that what is true for you in your private heart is true for all men:—that is genius. Speak your latent conviction, and it shall be the universal sense; for always the inmost becomes the outmost."
>EMERSON's Essay, "Self-Reliance."

"The difference between men is in their principle of association. Some men classify objects by color and size and other accidents of appearance; others by intrinsic likeness, or by the relation of cause and effect. The progress of the intellect consists in the clearer vision of causes, which over-

# Quotations and Suggestions 91

looks surface differences. To the poet, to the philosopher, to the saint, all things are friendly and sacred, all events profitable, all days holy, all men divine."

EMERSON'S Essay, "History."

"As you approximate to man's highest ideal of God, as your arm is strong and your knowledge is great, and the power to labor is with you, so shall you gain all that human heart desires.
*Story of an African Farm.*

"So nigh is grandeur to our dust,
   So near is God to man,
  When duty whispers low, 'Thou must!'
   The youth replies, 'I can.'"
EMERSON.

"It is we who may not cross over;
   Only with song and prayer,
  A little way into the glory
   We may reach as we leave her there.

"And somewhere yet, in the hilltops
   Of the country that hath no pain,

She will stand in her beautiful doorway
To give us her welcome again."

*Our Homemaker.*<br>Mrs. A. D. T. Whitney.

The sad part, to my mind, is not that we have, some of us, loved and lost, although that, indeed, is a bitter experience, but that we do not "reach," and look, toward and unto that "little way into the glory" which is permitted to those who climb to the top, to those who refuse to be discouraged by temporary disadvantages and hindrances.

*Fate.*

These withered hands are weak,
  But they shall do my bidding, though so frail,
  These lips are thin and white, yet shall not fail
The appointed words to speak.

Thy sneer I can forgive,
  Because I know the strength of destiny,

Until my task is done, I cannot die,
And then I would not live.
>                    JOHN A. DORGAN.

What an error to think that because we must bear suffering we should be sad! What an error to fail to face the future cheerfully and hopefully, even if it seem dark!

After all, there is little which can be said to advantage beyond Dr. Munger's words, when he says: "One thing you can do, and it is the best thing any man can do, you can keep up good heart."

And he adds: "This is courage, indeed, to look into a dull future and smile; to stay bound and not chafe under the cords; to endure pain and keep the cheer of health; to see hopes die out and not sink into brutish despair. Here is courage before which we may well pause with reverence and admiration. It is so high that we link it with divine things, carrying it quite beyond the sphere of any earthly success."

Not to shrink and turn back, not to turn away one's head and forget, but to "look" and "smile," smile because you have found that which is superior to dullness, that which can and will overcome!

Not to stay bound unwisely, or unnecessarily, but while bound avoiding chafing, and only when allowed making a break for something better.

"For something better than she had known," to any extent, or for any length of time! That is our desire, in the present and hereafter, "for something better," better than the ordinary, better than the practical, better than the physical, something more nearly perfect, more harmonious, and more complete! And to this desire has come and will come a sufficient answer.

### *Graceland's Graves.*

A peaceful city lies over there;
Never a heartache, never a care:
  No more longing for better days

Nor fruitless striving for higher ways,
At peace with the world, at rest with God;
Home once more to the kindly sod
   Where roses bloom and the fresh grass waves
   A gladsome vigil o'er Graceland's graves.

Some summer morning when skies are bright,—
Some night in winter when snows are white;
   It matters little the place nor when
   We shall have done with the cares of men:
Follow we must where our fathers led
Into the mystery of the dead,
   Seeking the peace the spirit craves;
   Choosing a home 'mid Graceland's graves.

No one knows of the burdens borne
Nor the cruel weight of yokes we've worn!
   The broken idols are all our own:
   The lips have smiled when the heart would moan:
Each one playing his dreary part;
Hiding the dead hopes in the heart;

We come to the stilling of the waves
And sunset leaves us at Graceland's graves.

And when we are gone from the haunts of men,
Will the world hold less of sunshine then?
Will mother, sister, sweetheart, wife,
Love more of eternity, less of life!
Are we building a palace high and grand,
Or a dingy hovel upon the sand?
So we ask the heart as the spirit craves
The answer waiting at Graceland's graves.

NIXON WATERMAN,
in *The Electric Spark.*

(Used by permission.)

Would it not have been more true, if the word "destined" had been used in the third verse, instead of "dreary"?

*Religion.*

We have before us the question of accepting and developing, or rejecting and contracting, what Lew Wallace speaks of as "the beautiful, pure life of the soul." And

# Quotations and Suggestions

in another part of that same wonderful book (*Ben-Hur*), he uses the wording, " Religion, which has, in its purity, but three elements, —God, the Soul, and their mutual recognition."

And what have "theologians" done for us, as to these " elements "? Too often have they taught us that we are, in our younger days, but unregenerate creatures, and must experience a change of heart, or must be born again, or, at least, must believe in their " theory," before we can be saved.

'T is false, this " theory " of theirs! We are created pure, and the " falling from grace " comes in by degrees, in our natural lives, by our own acts and through our own development or lack of development. We find, it is true, natural tendencies to evil, yet our spirits themselves are pure, and only become sullied by the continual choice of or love of the grosser, and indulgence of appetite.

The simple lines quoted below contain a great truth, for all who are willing to so live :

> "Keep innocence, be all a true man ought;
> Let neither pleasure tempt nor pain appal;
> Who hath this, he hath all things, having nought.
> Who hath it not hath nothing, having all."

Is it an easy thing to keep innocence? Does one happen to be all a true man ought? No, surely not! To fulfil these ideals requires continual attention to the truth.

"But," some one may ask, "is this religion?" Indeed it is, and the truest kind, for what can bear a better witness to the truth than the life itself, and what was Christ's own mission but, as He expressed it, "to bear witness to the truth"?

### *Sacrifice.*

As to lesser things, let them go, because thoroughly believing that the comparatively unimportant must be left out of our programmes of life! And by the comparatively unimportant we mean that which is less worth winning, less worth accomplishing.

# Quotations and Suggestions

As we go on in life we find that there are but a few things really worth winning. Few things that we accomplish are worth their price. But Oh, these "few things"! They are so rich in blessing, so true in effect, so much more than "worth while," that money, vital energy, position, yes, even happiness and life itself seem but small things as compared to them.

What, after all, is one human life? How many of them do we hear about, and know about, every day, as being wasted or sacrificed for lesser pleasures, or for cheap ambitions, by the ones directly concerned or by those who think they will be benefited by the sacrifice of some one else?

What are these "few things"? Part of them are suggested by William Watson's words, "loftier virtue, wisdom, courage, power," but *more* of them are included in the words, *truth and God*.

THE END.

# ONE MAN'S THESIS

## BY JOHN O. COIT

### Author of "Inspirations"

### PRICE, 50 CENTS

---

## PRESS NOTICES OF "ONE MAN'S THESIS."

Los Angeles, Cal., *Times.*—"This is a well-written little volume, full of pure devotional thought and helpful suggestiveness. The following is a sample of its teachings. "Our actions, our relations to others in this life, are, necessarily quite limited, but our spirits can be generous—our sympathies may be almost boundless, if we will."

Santa Barbara *Press.*—"A neat little volume published by Mr. John O. Coit, whose "Inspirations" were so well received a short time ago. The devotional tone that was one of the characteristics of his first book is equally strong in this later one, and a mingling of choice prose and poetry throughout the volume presents some very pleasurable and beneficial reading. The spirit of the book is uplifting, and the author may rest assured of finding a ready acceptance for this and any other of his works that he may give to the public."

Litchfield, Conn., *Enquirer.*—"John O. Coit, now once again of Litchfield, lately of Santa Barbara, Cal., has been so much encouraged by the success of his first literary venture, "Inspirations," that he has just published another interesting little book called "One Man's Thesis." While the tone of the selections is as pure and inspiring as in the first book, we think that in its literary merit "One Man's Thesis" is considerably ahead of "Inspirations," and we heartily congratulate Mr. Coit."

Boston, Mass., *Post-Courier.*—"A thoughtful exhortation in prose and verse, under several heads, to reach the higher life. It is highly devotional, pure and elevated in thought and cannot fail to be helpful in times of spiritual depression. The attractive form in which the matter is arranged makes it very readable."

Kansas City *Times.*—"A little volume deeply religious in tone and helpful to all who are trying to solve the problems of life through faith and hope."

www.ingramcontent.com/pod-product-compliance
Lightning Source LLC
Chambersburg PA
CBHW020153170426
**43199CB00010B/1012**